SongStream 2

An American Journey

10 Songs for Youth Choirs

Compiled and Edited by

Bob Chilcott & Peter Hunt

MUSIC DEPARTMENT

OXFORD
UNIVERSITY PRESS

OXFORD
UNIVERSITY PRESS

Great Clarendon Street, Oxford OX2 6DP, England
198 Madison Avenue, New York, NY, 10016, USA

Oxford University Press is a department of the University of Oxford.
It furthers the University's aim of excellence in research, scholarship,
and education by publishing worldwide

Oxford is a registered trade mark of Oxford University Press
in the UK and in certain other countries

1 3 5 7 9 10 8 6 4 2

ISBN 0-19-335572-8   978-0-19-335572-9

Music origination by Barnes Music Engraving Ltd., East Sussex
Printed in Great Britain on acid-free paper by
Halstan & Co. Ltd., Amersham, Bucks.

Contents

Performance Notes

by Bob Chilcott & Peter Hunt

1. Amazing Grace

This arrangement breaks out of the usual 3/4 mould and has an energetic gospel shuffle feel, reflecting the joy of the text which is about overcoming obstacles and striving to do better in your life. The strongest feature is the syncopated rhythms which must be relaxed and swing along with a legato feel, emphasizing the words as in natural speech. On the syncopated melismas (e.g. bar 21) slightly emphasize the first note, than back off. The vocal style should be bright, with an energetic tone and minimal vibrato, but do warm the tone towards the end of longer and sustained notes—particularly in unison or less dense passages. Singers must strive for the mature sound in their own voices, without forcing it or attempting to sound beyond their years. The 'shout chorus' in bars 75 to 92 presents an opportunity for a soulful soloist to embellish the written soprano line or improvise independently, in which case move the sopranos to the alto line for this passage. The opening eight bars should be full and robust before changing style in bar 9. **PH**

2. Buffalo Gals

I first wrote 'Buffalo Gals' in 1998 for the Highland Park High School Lads and Lassies in Dallas, Texas. Originally for SATB voices, it is presented here for SAB. The music is fast-moving and the colours change quickly, so each verse needs a good sense of character. The men believe without a doubt that they are there to be appreciated by the women, but the women are well aware of this! Sing the text with a lot of energy and personality, and try and keep the rhythm constant. Try practising bars 32–5 slowly at first, then little by little increase the speed until you get up to tempo. As you get faster and faster, sing it softer and softer! Most importantly, have fun with this piece, and perform it like a little drama! **BC**

3. Erosion

Eleanor Daley originally wrote 'Erosion' as a unison piece for Susan Knight and the choir at St Mary's School. The text is by E. J. Pratt, a prominent Newfoundland poet, and speaks of Newfoundland folks whose lives are ruled and changed by the sea. In the piano accompaniment you can hear the constant ebb and flow of the waves. Newfoundland has a robust climate and beautiful and dramatic landscapes. It is also the first land-mass you reach when travelling west across the Atlantic from Europe, so many people travel and have travelled through, bringing with them their different influences and characters. When singing this piece have in mind not only the strength of the environment of Newfoundland, but also the warmth of the people that make up this beautiful island community. **BC**

4. El Gavilán (The Sparrow-hawk)

This lively, quirky, and fun song features characteristic Latin-American rhythms with a percussive feel, forming a kind of vocal tapestry. The text should be sung in Spanish up to bar 20 and from bar 38, with the option of singing the English words in between. The constant quaver (eighth note) pulse is divided into 6/8 and 3/4 cross-rhythms. Practise this first with clapping and singing exercises, then to establish the style learn the main melody in soprano bars 20–28 (repeated baritone bars 28–34), perhaps first to 'da' to encourage a staccato and rhythmic sound—words can come later! None of the parts is difficult so practise slowly then piece them together. Aim for clarity of texture—keep each part light, using dynamics and letting notes go—and try to make the rhythms sound easy and natural. Aim for an extrovert and humorous quality.

To help with learning, divide the piece into five sections. Bars 5–20 include simple and repetitive motivic phrases, while bars 20–38 are the verses. Bars 38–54 may be sung with slides connecting the notes. Have fun and try to sound like calling birds, but don't lose the sense of rhythm. In bars 55–70 try to sound like percussive guitars and string basses; keep it light, and use the 'l' to articulate the rhythm. Bars 70–86 repeat bars 38–54. The whole song repeats from bar 20; if this is too long, perform one verse and add the other another year! **PH**

5. The Pessimist
This piece combines an original text by the American poet Benjamin Franklin King (which I have adapted slightly) with the 'Easy Winners' rag by Scott Joplin. Joplin's style is quite restrained, so the piece needs to be sung not only with irony but also very precisely, in a controlled and clear way. Don't try to sing this piece too fast. **BC**

6. Les Raftsmen
This lively song about woodsmen in the Ottawa valley dates from the mid-nineteenth century. The men would travel upstream by canoe and work through the winter months, then in the spring float the logs downstream in rafts. Bytown, where they would shop, is the original name for Ottawa.

This song needs to be sung with flair, in a muscular and positive style and with strength in the rhythms. The French text is very simple and includes some English words, so if you can sing in the original language, so much the better. The hand claps and thigh slaps add to the character of the piece and should be done positively. For extra character, add spoons! The 'mouth music' section at bar 37 recalls the practise of improvising nonsense syllables to mimic the sounds of other instruments. **BC**

7. Señora Santa Ana
On the surface this is a typical lullaby—simple melody, lilting rhythm, and gently encouraging words—but the verse/chorus structure and unusual minor 7th leap (e.g. bar 9) lift it out of the ordinary. The text interested me; the notion of an old man (the sandman) coming to take baby away presents a disturbing image, and is possibly a metaphor for a step into the unknown, or even death. The unsettled harmonies in the piano reflect this tension, while the voices from bar 39 to the end are confidently in F major.

The piece should be sung with gentle intensity throughout, with a warm vocal tone and legato line that follows the natural rise and fall of the phrases. The baritones must support their tone from bar 39 to stay in tune, and the piano can help quietly if required. The English translation is very singable, but challenge singers with the Spanish—it's not difficult. In any case, sing 'Duérmase niño' at the end, pronounced *dwair-masser knee-nyo*. Can you spot the reference to a nursery rhyme in bars 30–35?! **PH**

8. Take flight
This is a wonderfully uplifting song full of pace and energy, about trying new wings in new skies, and going for the future! It requires a light, easy singing style; the words should be well focused with crisp consonants, but without working too hard, and the rhythms should be relaxed and sound natural. The tempo should be a fast three, or one-in-a-bar if possible. Practise speaking the verses quietly to establish the style, then add the pitches and get it really secure before adding the accompaniment. Enjoy the chorus; crescendo to the word 'flight' each time and aim for an open, rounded vowel. The 'middle eight' (bar 65) should start quietly with a well-controlled crescendo to 'soar' in bar 73. Faces should be bright and shining throughout, radiating optimism. **PH**

9. Wanting Memories

Ysaye M. Barnwell is a singer–composer and a long-time member of the acclaimed African-American vocal sextet Sweet Honey In The Rock. 'Wanting Memories' is recorded on the group's 1993 album *Still on the Journey*. I first performed this piece with the BBC Singers, and it has become a firm favourite of theirs. The bass part should be unforced and almost mantra-like, while the upper voices need to shape each phrase carefully and sing the beautiful lyrics expressively. When singing in harmony, take care that all parts are shaped and phrased the same way, and let the lyrics have a natural flow. Aim for a yearning quality in the singing—expressive, but not forced—and be careful not to rush; everyone needs to feel the pulse. I have added a simple dynamic scheme to help give the piece shape, and also suggested suitable places to breathe. **BC**

10. Wayfarin' Stranger

This simple and expressive folk hymn has here been given fresh treatment by the addition of a funky and lively piano part, suggesting underlying hope and optimism about moving on. Strong and assertive singing is required, and voices need to grow in volume and intensity through the long notes in each phrase. The few syncopations must be punchy and rhythmic to match the piano. Relax the tone in bar 50 without losing the intensity—keep it supported—and ensure that the baritones clip their rhythm neatly in bar 57 with a staccato 'keep' before exploding with energy in bar 58! For variety at the end, try going very quiet, or feature just a few voices (or solo); keep the 'o' on the last long note focused with a darkish tone, and perhaps close onto the 'm' and hum the last two bars. **PH**

1. Amazing Grace

John Newton (1725–1807)

American folk melody
arr. STEVEN MILLOY

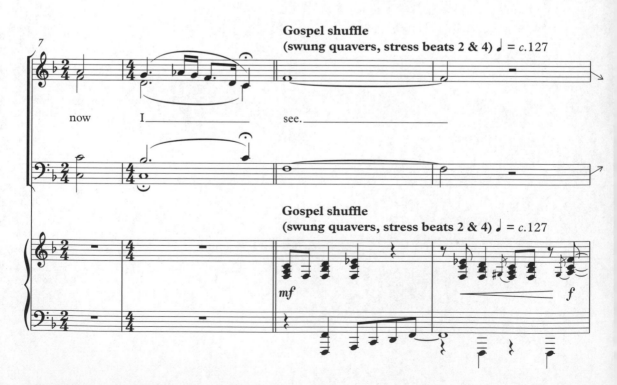

2. Buffalo Gals

American Traditional
arr. **BOB CHILCOTT**

This arrangement for SAB voices has been adapted from the original SATB version 0–19–343231–5 / 978–0–19–343231–4.

way - oh, way way-oh

As

I was walk - ing down the street, down the street, down the street, a

hand - some girl I chanced to meet, oh she was fair to see.

come out to-night? come out to-night? Buf-fa-lo Gals won't you come out to-night and

-night? come out to-night? come out to-night? Buf-fa-lo Gals won't you come out to -

dance by the light of the moon?

-night and dance by the light of the moon?

mf

p

Oh, I danced with the gal with a hole in her stock-in' and her

p

sfz *p*

for Susan Knight

3. Erosion

E. J. Pratt (1882–1964)

ELEANOR DALEY

* stagger breathing

* stagger breathing

* stagger breathing

4. El Gavilán
(The Sparrow-hawk)

Venezuelan Traditional
arr. **ALBERTO GRAU**

pío and *tao* represent the sounds made by the gavilán, or sparrow-hawk.

carrao a Venezuelan bird that lives in estuary habitats

5. The Pessimist
(Easy Winners)

With apologies to
Benjamin Franklin King (1857–1894)

SCOTT JOPLIN
arr. BOB CHILCOTT

44

tick-le my brain, no-thing to get me out of bed,_ I'm go-ing in-sane, it's

I'm go-ing in-sane,_

do-ing in my head, and may-be they just think I'm la - zy,

_ and may-be, and may - be

well, that's a - no - ther thing that

6. Les Raftsmen

Trad.
English text: Bob Chilcott

Québecois Traditional
arr. **MARK SIRETT**

bang sur la ring, bang sur la ring,_____ lais - sez pas - ser
bang on the wood, *bang on the wood,*_____ *let the rafts - men*

les rafts - men, bang sur la ring, bang sur la ring,
go up - stream, *bang on the wood,* *bang on the wood,*

bang sur la ring,_____ bing, bang!_____
*bang on the wood,*_____ *bing, bang!*_____

7. Señora Santa Ana

Mexican lullaby
arr. **PETER HUNT**

Duér-ma - se, ni - ño, duér-ma - se ya, que ahí vie-ne el vie-jo y se
Sleep now, my ba - by, sleep now I pray. An old man is com-ing to

lo lle-va - rá. que ahí vie-ne el vie-jo y se lo lle-va - rá.
take you a - way. old man is com-ing to take you a - way.

Du - ér - ma-se, ni - ño,
Close your eyes, my ba - by,

Du - ér - ma-se,
Close your eyes, my

Ni - ño, ni - ño,
Ni - ño, ni - ño,

Duér - ma - se, ni - ño, duér - ma - se ya,___ que ahí vie - ne el vie - jo y se
Sleep now, my ba - by, sleep now I pray.___ An old man is com - ing to

(2nd time only)

lo lle - va - rá.   **lo lle - va - rá.**   **Duér - ma - se, ni -**
take you a - way.   *take you a - way.*

Duér - ma - se,

Duér - ma - se, ni - ño,

-ño, duér - ma - se, ni - ño, duér - ma - se, ni - ño.

ni - ño, duér - ma - se, ni - ño.

duér - ma - se, ni - ño, duér - ma - se, ni - ño.   **Oh**

to the Parkway South Vocal Music Department and their Director, Ronna Paden

8. Take flight

Michael Roth
additional lyrics Steven Milloy

STEVEN MILLOY

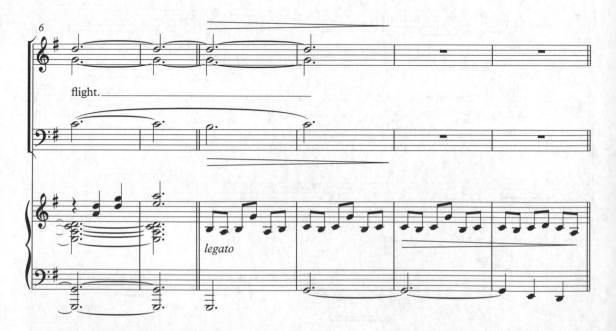

verse 1: **TUTTI**
verse 2: **SOLO** or **SOLI**

1. I've
2. I

(verse 2 only)

Take

(verse 2 only)

grown ac-cus-tomed to the feel_ of this fam-il - iar__ place and
knew the day_ I'd have to say good-bye was draw-ing__ near. Now,

flight.

I've got to leave this place be - hind
The urge would be__ so strong to__ go!

'cause there is a sky I long to try; it's
How can I stay bound here on the ground, when

say - ing, 'You can fly!'__ 'Take_
I hear a voice re - sound:__

-on   the   wind,   take   flight.'

-on   the   wind,   take   flight.'

take   flight.'

And if I'm bold e - nough and ask for more,   not

9. Wanting Memories
(from *Crossings*)

Words and Music
YSAYE M. BARNWELL

SOPRANO

MELODY

ALTO

BASS

doom doom doom_ doom_ doom   doom   doom   doom_   doom_ doom

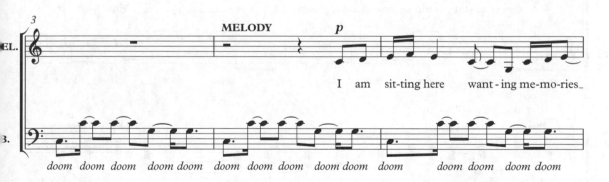

EL.

MELODY *p*

I am sit-ting here   want-ing me-mo-ries_

B.

doom doom doom doom doom   doom doom doom doom doom   doom   doom doom doom doom

_ to teach me_ to see the beau-ty in the world through my own_ eyes._____ Yes, I am

doom   doom   doom   doom doom   doom   doom   doom_   doom   doom   doom doom doom   doom doom

Dynamics and breathing suggestions are editorial.

com - fort me in times like these and now I need you,___ and now I

doom doom doom___ doom___ doom doom doom doom___ doom___ doom

need you,_____ and you are___ gone.

need you,_____ and you are___ gone._____

doom doom doom doom doom doom doom doom doom doom doom doom doom doom doom

_____ So, I am sit - ting here want - ing me - mo - ries___

So, I am

I am sit - ting here want - ing me - mo - ries___

shay-kah shay-kah shay-kah shay-kah

doom doom doom___ doom___ doom doom doom doom___ doom___ doom

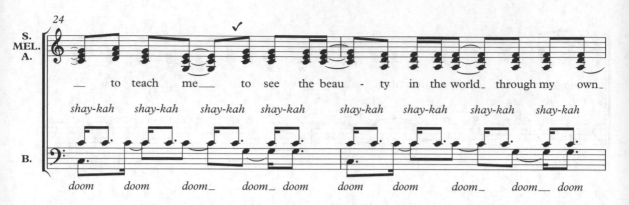

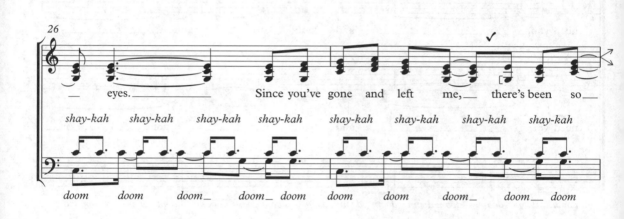

40

Yes, I am sit - ting here want - ing me - mo - ries__

Yes, I am

I am sit - ting here want - ing me - mo - ries__

shay-kah shay-kah shay-kah shay-kah

doom doom doom__ doom__ doom doom doom doom__ doom__ doom

42

S.
MEL.
A.

__ to teach me__ to see the beau - ty in the world__ through my own__

shay-kah shay-kah shay-kah shay-kah shay-kah shay-kah shay-kah shay-kah

B.

doom doom doom__ doom__ doom doom doom doom__ doom__ doom

44

1.

__ eyes.____ Yes, I am

2.

__ eyes.__ I think on the things that

shay-kah shay-kah shay-kah shay-kah shay-kah shay-kah shay-kah shay-kah

doom doom doom__ doom__ doom doom doom doom__ doom__ doom

made me feel_ so won - der-ful when I was young,_____ I think on the things that

doom doom doom doom_ doom doom doom doom_ doom_ doom

made me laugh, made me dance, made me sing,_____ I think on the things that

doom doom doom_ doom_ doom doom doom doom_ doom_ doom

made me grow in-to a be-ing full of pride; think on these_____ things,_____

doom doom doom doom doom doom doom doom doom doom doom doom doom doom doom

S.

_ for they are_____ truth._____ And I am

EL. A.

And I am

_ for they are_____ truth._____ I am

B.

doom doom doom doom doom doom doom doom doom doom doom doom doom doom doom

sit-ting here want-ing me-mo-ries to teach me to see the beau-

shay-kah shay-kah shay-kah shay-kah shay-kah shay-kah shay-kah shay-kah

doom doom doom doom doom doom doom doom doom doom

-ty in the world through my own eyes. I thought that

shay-kah shay-kah shay-kah shay-kah shay-kah shay-kah shay-kah I

doom doom doom doom doom doom doom doom doom doom

you were gone, but now I know you're with me; you are the

thought that you were gone, but now I know you're with me; you

doom doom doom doom doom doom doom doom doom doom

grain of sand,__ I know that I've been blessed a - gain and o - ver__

grain of sand,__ sand, sand,__ I know that I've__ been blessed

grain of sand, I know that I've been blessed a -

doom doom doom__ doom__ doom doom doom doom____ doom__ doom

dim.   *p*

a - gain._____ Yes, I am

dim.   *p*

__ a - gain and a-gain and a-gain.____ Yes, I am

dim.   *p*

a-gain and a-gain and a - gain._____ Yes, I am

dim.

- gain and o-ver a - gain and o - ver__ a - gain.____

dim.

doom doom doom doom doom doom doom doom__ doom doom doom doom doom doom doom

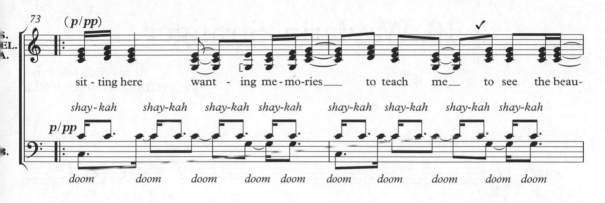

sit - ting here   want - ing me - mo - ries___ to teach   me___   to see   the beau-

shay-kah   shay-kah   shay-kah shay-kah   shay-kah   shay-kah   shay-kah shay-kah

doom   doom   doom   doom doom   doom   doom   doom   doom doom

- ty in the world through my own___ eyes.___   Yes, I am

shay-kah   shay-kah   shay-kah   shay-kah   shay-kah   shay-kah   shay-kah   shay-kah

doom   doom   doom___   doom___   doom   doom   doom   doom___   doom___   doom

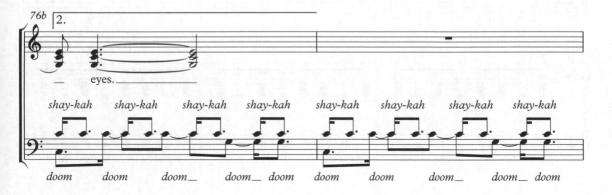

___ eyes.___

shay-kah   shay-kah   shay-kah   shay-kah   shay-kah   shay-kah   shay-kah   shay-kah

doom   doom   doom___   doom___   doom   doom   doom   doom___   doom___   doom

shay-kah   shay-kah   shay-kah   shay-kah

doom   doom   doom___   doom___   doom   doom   doom   doom___   doom___   doom

doom   doom   doom___   doom doom   doom   doom   doom___   doom doom   doom.

for the Shalom Choirs

10. Wayfarin' Stranger

Appalachian folk hymn
arr. **REGINALD UNTERSEHER**

I'm just a poor_____ way - far - in' stran - ger,

I'm go-in' there_____ no more to roam.

TUTTI

I'm on-ly go — — in' ov-er Jor-dan, I'm on-ly

go — — in' ov-er home._____